Climate Change

Chris Oxlade

W

FRANKLIN WATTS

LONDON•SYDNEY

First published in 2008 by Franklin Watts

Franklin Watts
338 Euston Road
London NW1 3BH

Franklin Watts Australia
Level 17/207 Kent Street
Sydney NSW 2000

Dewey number: 363.738'74

ISBN: 978 0 7496 8268 2

Printed in China

A CIP catalogue record for this book
is available from the British Library

Franklin Watts is a division of Hachette Children's Books,
an Hachette Livre UK company.

www.hachettelivre.co.uk

Editor: Sarah Ridley
Design: Billin Design Solutions
Editor in Chief: John C. Miles
Art Director: Jonathan Hair
Picture research: Diana Morris

Picture credits:
Greg Allen/Rex Features: 33b. Allover Norway/Rex Features: 23. Arctic Images/Corbis:
15b. Vera Bogaerts/Shutterstock: 8, 46-47. Gerard Cerlis /Getty Images: 22. W Perry
Conway/Corbis: 21. Mary Evans PL: 16. Factoria Singular Fotografia/Shutterstock: 29t.
Firefly Productions/Corbis: 19. Greenpeace: 24. Robert Harding/Getty Images: 10
Roman Kobzarev/Shutterstock: 17c. Peter Lawson/Rex Features: 33t. Lou Linwel/Rex
Features: 30, 35. Stephanie Maze/Corbis: 18. Louise Murray/SPL: cover t. NASA: 20c, 41.
Mosatoshi Okauchi/Rex Features: 38. Picturepoint/Topfoto: 14. Mark Ralston/AFP/Getty
Images: 31. Rex Features: 28, 37b. Ronen /Shutterstock: 1, 11b. David Rose/Panos
Pictures: 29b. Jewel Samad/Getty Images: 32. John Sartin/Shutterstock: 17t.
Sipa Press/Rex Features: cover b, 25, 27c, 27b, 34, 36, 37c, 40. Thoma/Shutterstock: 13.
Vera Tomankova/Shutterstock: 2-3, 5t, 7t, 9, 11t, 15t. World History Archive/Topfoto: 12.
Toru Yamanaka/AFP/Getty Images: 26.

CONTENTS

WHAT IS CLIMATE CHANGE?

▲ Climate change is causing Arctic ice to melt.

CLIMATE CHANGE is the change in the patterns of the world's weather. Climate change is already happening, and future change could lead to more severe weather events, and side effects such as sea-level rises and the spread of deserts. Climate change is one of the most pressing problems for the human race.

GRADUAL CHANGES

Climate is the pattern of weather (temperature, rainfall, and so on) that happens at a place over a long period of time. Although the weather changes from day to day, climate normally stays the same year after year. There are many different climates in different parts of the world. Climate change refers to the gradual changes in the different climates around the world.

CAUSES OF CLIMATE CHANGE

Climates have been changing naturally for millions of years, but most weather experts agree that the climate change we are seeing today is caused by human activities, mainly the build up in the atmosphere of carbon dioxide gas released by burning fossil fuels.

CLIMATE CHANGE IN THE NEWS

Climate change appears in the news almost daily. Every extreme weather event, such as a hurricane, drought, flood or fire, is linked to climate change, as are shrinking ice caps and glaciers. There is also wide coverage of climate-change summits and protests, and heated debates between environmentalists and climate-change sceptics.

GET THE FACTS STRAIGHT

- Since 1970, the average global surface temperature has risen by 0.5°C.

- Ten of the warmest years in the last hundred years occurred between 1990 and 2006.

- The level of carbon dioxide in the atmosphere has risen from 270 parts per million in pre-industrial days to 380 parts per million today.

- Average sea levels have risen by 20 cm in the last hundred years.

▼ Power-station chimneys pour carbon dioxide into the atmosphere.

9

CLIMATE CHANGE SCIENCE

ALL THE ENERGY that drives the Earth's weather comes from the Sun in the form of rays of light and heat. On average, about half the energy that hits the Earth is absorbed by the surface. The warmed surface then radiates the energy back into the atmosphere as heat. The rest of the energy from the Sun is reflected or absorbed by clouds and water vapour in the atmosphere, or is reflected by the Earth's surface.

▲ Hot desert areas radiate heat into the Earth's atmosphere like a domestic radiator.

THE GREENHOUSE EFFECT

Some of the energy the Earth radiates escapes into space, but most is absorbed by clouds and certain gases in the atmosphere. In turn, the clouds and gases radiate some of the energy back to the surface. In this way, heat is trapped in the lower atmosphere. This natural effect is called the greenhouse effect. It keeps the average air temperature across the surface of the Earth at about 14°C. Without the greenhouse effect, all the heat from the Earth would escape straight into space. The average temperature would be about −18°C, and life would probably not exist here.

GREENHOUSE GASES

The atmosphere is made up of a mixture of gases. About 99% is oxygen and nitrogen, but it is the small amounts of other gases that are responsible for the greenhouse effect.

The main greenhouse gases are water vapour, carbon dioxide, methane, nitrous oxide and ozone (see pages 16-17). These gases have always been in the atmosphere, trapping heat. But because we are adding more of these gases to the atmosphere, the greenhouse effect is becoming more intense, and more heat is being trapped than before. So the average global temperature is rising. This is known as global warming. The increasing heat is causing climate change.

GET THE FACTS STRAIGHT

Carbon cycles naturally between the atmosphere, the oceans, the soil and plants.

- Plants take in carbon dioxide during photosynthesis, and the carbon is trapped in their tissues.

- When plants die and rot away, the carbon is released again as carbon dioxide.

- About half the carbon dioxide we put into the atmosphere is taken up by plants and the oceans. These are known as carbon sinks.

▲ The world's rainforests are carbon sinks because new growth takes up some of the carbon dioxide in the atmosphere.

CLIMATE SCIENCE HISTORY

IN THE 1820s, French scientist Joseph Fourier (1768-1830) realised that our atmosphere traps some heat, keeping us warm. He likened the effect to a greenhouse. In the next decade, the Swiss-born American Louis Agassiz (1807-1873) introduced the idea of ice ages (see pages 14-15), showing that the Earth's climates have been different in the past.

▲ Svante Arrhenius was the first scientist to link carbon dioxide with climate change.

MAKING A LINK

Swedish scientist Svante Arrhenius (1859-1927) made the link between the ice ages and the level of carbon dioxide in the atmosphere. He calculated that if the level of carbon dioxide was halved, the temperature would drop by 5°C, and if it was doubled, the temperature would rise by 5°C. Other scientists thought there was little chance of human activities affecting the climate.

MODERN MEASUREMENTS

Scientists started measuring the levels of different atmospheric gases in 1958. As the years passed, they detected carbon dioxide levels rising. The first computer climate models were designed in the 1960s, and they showed that increased carbon dioxide levels would warm the atmosphere. Then in the 1980s, weather data confirmed that the average global temperature was rising.

A LANDMARK YEAR

In 1988, the USA experienced a hot, dry summer, with devastating forest fires. In the same year, NASA scientist James Hansen told the US Congress he was almost certain that human-induced climate change had arrived. The floodgates had opened. Today, it is not a question of whether climate change is happening, but to what degree it is happening, and what will happen in the future.

▲ Atmospheric carbon dioxide levels have been measured at the observatory on Hawaii since 1958.

WHAT DO YOU THINK?

Climate change stories first appeared regularly in the news in 1988, after James Hansen's speech, but they died away until the second half of the 1990s.

- How would you have reacted as a journalist in 1988? Would you have let the story die away?

- Why do you think climate-change stories did die away for a while?

CLIMATE CHANGE IN THE PAST

CLIMATE CHANGE may be a new phenomenon for us, but it's not for the Earth, or even for humans. It has been happening naturally for billions of years, ever since the Earth was formed. These climate changes were caused by natural cycles, such as changes in the Earth's orbit around the Sun, and changes in the amount of energy the Sun emits.

▲ During the Little Ice Age, winters in London were cold enough for the River Thames to freeze over.

CLIMATE HISTORY

In the time since the Earth was formed 4,500 million years ago, climates have been very different from today. Generally, the temperature was several degrees warmer than today, but in the last 1,000 million years, the warmth was interrupted by cold periods. The last of these started about two million years ago and finished only about 14,000 years ago. During this last period, much of the northern hemisphere was periodically covered with deep ice sheets. These periods are called ice ages. The temperature has fluctuated a few degrees up and down since the end of the last ice age. For instance, the period from 1550 to 1850 is known as the Little Ice Age because cold winters were more common than today.

EVIDENCE FOR CLIMATE CHANGE

Three main types of evidence tell us what the climate was like hundreds, thousands, and even millions of years ago.

- Accurate weather records taken over the last few centuries.

- Historical documents, such as descriptions of thick ice on the River Thames in London hundreds of years ago.

- Evidence from the Earth itself. For example, analysis of gas bubbles trapped deep in ice sheets tells us what the atmosphere was like thousands of years ago.

WHAT DO YOU THINK?

- Can we rely on written records from long ago to tell us what climate was like?

- Is a single weather event evidence for climate change?

▼ A scientist examines layers of ice in a core taken from the Greenland ice cap.

CAUSES OF CLIMATE CHANGE

WHAT ARE THE CAUSES of the climate change that is happening today? Number one on the list is our addition of greenhouse gases (mainly carbon dioxide and methane) to the atmosphere, which is trapping more of the Sun's heat in the atmosphere.

CARBON DIOXIDE CONCENTRATIONS

Climate change is a consequence of the industrial age. When the Industrial Revolution began in the 18th century, the concentration of carbon dioxide in the atmosphere was 280 parts per million (ppm), or 0.028%. Ice-core analysis shows that it had been at this level for at least 800 years. Today, the concentration is 380 ppm. Each year, we add an extra 30 billion tonnes of carbon dioxide to the 3,000 billion tonnes already in the atmosphere.

METHANE

There is far less methane (only 2 ppm) in the atmosphere than carbon dioxide, but methane traps heat much better. Since 1750, its concentration in the atmosphere has risen by 150%. Sources of methane are rice farming, grazing animals (as they digest grass), mining operations and drilling for gas and oil (when methane escapes from underground) and decomposing waste in landfill sites.

◀ The Industrial Revolution of the 18th and 19th centuries heralded the beginning of the rise in carbon dioxide levels.

▲ Rice growing releases methane as vegetation rots under water.

◄ Cattle produce methane as they digest grass.

MORE GREENHOUSE GASES

Other greenhouse gases are chlorofluorocarbons, nitrous oxide and ozone. Chlorofluorocarbons are powerful greenhouse gases. They were used mainly as refrigerants but they are used less now as they were responsible for making a hole in the ozone layer – part of the Earth's atmosphere. Nitrous oxide comes from fossil fuels, but mostly from fertilizers. Ozone is formed in smog from burning fossil fuels.

GET THE FACTS STRAIGHT

Gases are not the only players in the greenhouse effect. Aerosols, which are extremely small particles, also affect how heat from the Sun is trapped.

- Sulphate aerosol from fossil fuels reflects sunlight, so it reduces global warming.

- Carbon particles from fossil fuels trap heat, and are responsible for about 7% of global warming.

CARBON DIOXIDE EMISSIONS

FOSSIL FUELS – coal, oil and gas – contain chemicals called hydrocarbons. When these burn, they create heat and form carbon dioxide and water. Fossil fuels are burned in power stations, in vehicle, aircraft and ship engines, in domestic heating systems, and in many other places. Emissions from burning fossil fuels are responsible for more than three-quarters of all the carbon dioxide we put into the Earth's atmosphere.

MORE SOURCES OF CARBON DIOXIDE

Most of the rest of the carbon dioxide we add to the atmosphere comes from changing land use, such as deforestation, draining bogs and clearing vegetation to grow crops. Deforestation is the main culprit. As temperatures rise, the world's permafrost will melt, releasing carbon dioxide and methane.

▼ In the developing world, vegetation clearance by burning pumps carbon dioxide into the Earth's atmosphere.

▶ Jet aircraft engines are one of the biggest producers of carbon dioxide emissions today.

CARBON FOOTPRINTS

A carbon footprint is the amount of carbon dioxide emissions that a person or organisation is responsible for. A carbon footprint takes into account energy used at home and energy used in transport. In western countries, this "personal footprint" is about half a person's overall footprint.

The rest comes from energy used at work or school, by governments, and in the production of things, including food.

The average western European has a carbon footprint of about 12 tonnes of carbon dioxide per year. Americans and Australians have footprints of about 20 tonnes per year. In developing countries, relatively few people have cars or electrical goods. Their carbon footprints are much lower than people in developed countries. The world average carbon footprint is about four tonnes per year.

WHAT DO YOU THINK?

One twelfth of the world's population is responsible for half the world's carbon emissions.

● Why do people in richer nations have larger carbon footprints than people in developing countries?

● Is it fair that some people have larger carbon footprints than others?

THE EFFECTS OF CLIMATE CHANGE

MEASUREMENTS FROM HUNDREDS of weather stations around the world show that the average global air temperature at the Earth's surface is 0.8°C higher in 2008 than it was a hundred years ago. In the oceans, the average temperature of the surface layer has increased by 0.3°C. Rainfall has also been affected. In the mid-latitudes, the number of times rainfall has lasted for five days or more has increased by about 5%.

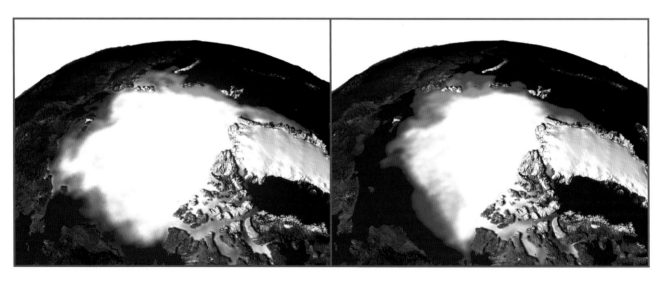

▲ These images show how the area of Arctic sea ice has shrunk between 1979 (left) and 2005 (right) due to global temperature rises.

EXTREME WEATHER

The last few years have seen an increase in the number and severity of extreme weather events. In summer 2003, a heat wave hit Europe, bringing record high temperatures in several cities, and destroying crops in southern Europe. The number of very powerful hurricanes in the Atlantic has increased since the 1970s, probably as a result of increased ocean temperatures. The World Health Organization estimates that 150,000 people have died as a result of climate change, including 20,000 lives in the 2003 European heat wave.

PHYSICAL EVIDENCE

Measurements show that, on average, the world's glaciers have shortened by a kilometre in the last hundred years. In the Arctic, the ice cap is smaller in midwinter than it used to be because higher temperatures slow the rate at which the sea freezes over. Average sea levels have risen between 10 cm and 20 cm over the last century, mainly because the water has expanded as it has warmed.

▼ Polar bears are losing their habitat as Arctic ice retreats.

FACING THE ISSUES

Changing temperatures have affected many animals' habitats. Mosquitoes are thriving further north than before, and the growing season is becoming longer in the northern hemisphere.

The polar bear has become a popular symbol of climate change. It is losing its seal-hunting grounds as Arctic sea ice shrinks, and is increasingly scavenging in towns around the Arctic Circle.

CLIMATE CHANGE REPORTS

MANY REPORTS on climate change come from official weather and climate services, such as the NOAA in the USA and the Meteorological Office in the UK. However, the most influential climate reports have come from the Intergovernmental Panel on Climate Change (IPCC).

▲ IPCC delegates regularly meet to discuss the problems of climate change.

FACING THE ISSUES

In 2006, one of the UK's leading economists, Sir Nicholas Stern, published a report on the cost of climate change. It concluded that the effects of climate change could cost £3.7 trillion (£3.7 million million) in the UK alone – far more than the cost of combating climate change would be.

THE IPCC

The IPCC was formed in 1988 by the World Meteorological Organization (WMO) and the United Nations Environment Programme (UNEP). Its job is to evaluate scientific evidence on climate change and report on it. The IPCC has a number of different groups of scientists, called working groups, that write assessments on different aspects of climate change. One group reports on the physical evidence for climate change, another on how we can deal with its effects, and another on how we can combat climate change. The assessments are written and reviewed by hundreds of climate experts, giving the IPCC assessments great authority.

▼ Dr Rajendra Pachauri accepts the Nobel Peace Prize on behalf of the IPCC, Oslo, Norway, 2007.

IPCC ASSESSMENTS

The first IPCC assessment, published in 1990, discussed the dangers of global warming. The second, published in 1995, concluded: "The balance of evidence suggests a discernible human influence on global climates." This assessment was a driving force behind the Kyoto Protocol (see page 26). In the third report, published in 2001, the IPCC concluded that: "There is new and stronger evidence that most of the warming observed over the last 50 years is attributable to human activities." The latest assessment was published in 2007. It predicts that global temperatures will rise between 1.5°C (with low emissions) and 6°C (with high emissions) by 2100, and warns that a 25% to 40% cut in emissions is needed by 2020 to avert major climate change.

PIONEER PRESSURE GROUPS

ENVIRONMENTAL PRESSURE GROUPS

such as Friends of the Earth and Greenpeace were formed in the early 1970s. This was before the issue of climate change was in the news. At the time, these pressure groups raised awareness of pollution from fossil fuels, but not carbon emissions in particular. There were also grave concerns about a nuclear war between western countries and the Soviet Union, which would lead to global cooling known as a nuclear winter.

EARLY PROTESTS

Climate change hit the news in the late 1980s. By then, the major environmental pressure groups were well known. They quickly began to push climate change into the limelight, especially in North America and Europe.

In 1992, thousands of activists from pressure groups all over the world journeyed to the Earth Summit in Rio de Janeiro, Brazil, to raise awareness of climate change.

▲ Greenpeace was formed in 1971, when its activists fought successfully against nuclear weapons tests in Alaska. This is one of their early anti-nuclear demonstrations.

▲ Activists protesting against the environmental policies of the US government of US President George W Bush at the Earth Summit in Rio de Janeiro in 1992.

FACING THE ISSUES

In the late 1980s and the 1990s, a few scientists who were funded by western governments reported that they were "gagged". They were not allowed to publish their findings on climate change, were forced to water down their warnings, or had to allow higher authorities to edit their scientific papers.

OPPOSITE PRESSURES

Climate change protests were not all from environmental groups. In the late 1980s, and through the 1990s, industrialists pressurised governments too, saying that forcing people to use less fossil fuels would result in economic disaster. Oil companies and car manufacturers exerted the greatest pressure, since they would have had the most to lose. In the 1990s, a group called the Global Climate Coalition, made up of several global oil companies and manufacturing companies, represented industrialists at climate conferences. Their cause was helped by scientists who were sceptical about climate change, and who were often funded by the industrialists. They were a powerful voice against climate change in the media.

CLIMATE-CHANGE SUMMITS

SINCE THE EARLY 1990s

there has been a series of international climate-change summits, attended by delegates from the world's governments, scientific experts and various pressure groups. At the 1992 Rio de Janeiro Earth Summit governments pledged to prevent dangerous climate change, and signed the United Nations Framework Convention on Climate Change.

THE KYOTO PROTOCOL

In 1997, delegates met in Kyoto, Japan, to discuss the threat of climate change. After many days of negotiations, nearly all countries signed up to a climate-change treaty called the Kyoto Protocol. Forty industrialised countries promised that they would cut their greenhouse gas emissions to below 1990 levels by 2012. The Protocol came into force in 2005. Developing countries also signed the treaty, but they were not required to reduce their emissions. The USA and Australia signed the Kyoto Protocol, but then backed out, mainly because they did not agree that developing countries should have no emission targets.

◄ A protestor's message board at a rally during the Kyoto conference in 1997.

AFTER KYOTO

Governments met in 2007 in Bali, Indonesia, to plan a "road map" to a post-Kyoto Protocol. There were serious disagreements at Bali about the levels of emission cuts necessary. European governments wanted a promise of 25% to 40% cuts by 2020, as recommended by the IPCC, but the USA, along with Canada, Japan and Russia would not agree to put figures in the plan. After heated negotiations, agreement was reached to make "deep cuts" in emissions.

◀ UN Secretary-General Ban Ki-moon speaking at Bali.

▼ Delegates at the Bali summit in 2007.

GOVERNMENT REACTIONS

SOME COUNTRIES have signed up to substantial reductions in their carbon emissions as part of the Kyoto Protocol. Other countries set themselves much larger targets than agreed at Kyoto. Some have volunteered to make reductions when they can. Still others have decided to rely on the future development of low-carbon technologies.

▶ US President George W Bush was regularly criticized for his lack of commitment to climate-change policies.

AGAINST KYOTO

In 1997, the USA and Australia backed out of the Kyoto Protocol (see page 26). However, several American states, such as California and Texas, are setting their own emissions targets, and in 2007 the USA signed the "Bali road map" (see page 27). Australian ex-prime minister John Howard was a climate change sceptic, but new prime minister Kevin Rudd agreed to Kyoto in 2007, partly in response to Australia's worst drought in a century.

UK RESPONSE

After Kyoto, the UK set a target of a 20% reduction in emissions by 2010, and its new Climate Change Bill specifies a 60% cut by 2050. However, it is already struggling to meet the first of these targets. In 2007, emission reduction was one of the reasons that the UK decided to approve new nuclear power stations. Another UK idea is for people to carry emission "ration cards".

CARBON-TRADING

The Kyoto Protocol allows countries to trade emission allowances. So if a country emits less than its target, it can sell its extra allowance to another country. This has led to an international carbon-trading market. The UK idea for emission "ration cards", just mentioned, would give people a carbon-emission ration which would be used up when buying fuels or consumer goods.

GET THE FACTS STRAIGHT

- In Spain, all new buildings must use solar panels to provide some of their energy.

- In the UK, from the year 2015, all new homes must be "zero carbon", that is, they must produce no carbon emissions.

- The US government is funding companies to develop green technologies.

▲ Countries that use a lot of renewable energy, such as wind power, are able to sell their carbon credits.

◀ Sweden has invested in green ideas. In the town of Umea, cycling is encouraged, and waste from the timber industry is burned for heating and electricity generation.

NEW INDUSTRIAL NATIONS

CHINA AND INDIA will eventually overtake the USA to become the world's largest carbon emitters. Their emissions are rising as energy demand increases and economic success means people have more money to spend on appliances and travel.

CHINA'S GROWTH

China's overall carbon emissions are rising alarmingly quickly – in 2006, they rose by 8%. These increasing emissions are down to rapid growth in manufacturing industries in China. Two new coal-fired power stations open every week in China to provide electricity for this growth. If China's emissions continue to grow so fast, experts estimate that it will be responsible for a third of all the world's emissions by 2030.

▼ Emissions are growing as heavy industry expands in China.

東灘生态城市首期启动区面积为6.3平方公里，由三座相互连接的村庄组成
游、创新科技、以及健康为不同主题的混合功能开发区。首先动工的
里的居民能方便地搭乘公共交通工具，500米以内即可搭乘公交车
专用路线，穿过郁郁葱葱的绿色美景，步行或骑车去上班、购物或
了。无需奔波往返于上海市区。同时，这里还会成为上海附近极富吸

CHINA'S PLEDGES

China does not have to reduce emissions under the Kyoto Protocol. However, it has promised to improve its energy efficiency, and has published its own climate-change action plan. At Bali, China committed to "measurable, reportable and verifiable mitigation actions", so long as it had help from rich, already developed nations. Environmentalists accuse the Chinese government of deliberately underestimating its emission figures.

▲ China is planning new "green cities" to keep down its emissions. Here, architects discuss plans for a new city called Dongtan.

INDIAN EMISSIONS

Like China, India argues that the world's developed countries, which have created the problem of global warming, should take the main responsibility for fighting climate change. It argues that, per person, its emissions are less than a quarter of America's.

WHAT DO YOU THINK?

Developing countries argue that already industrialised countries have no right to tell them to reduce their carbon emissions. They also argue that their per capita emissions are far less than those of developed countries.

- Should the developing nations be allowed to increase emissions?
- Why should you bother to reduce your own emissions when your efforts are wiped out in seconds by emission increases in China?

CONTINUING PROTESTS

THE MAJORITY of governments and people around the world now accept that climate change is happening, and that they need to take action against it. However, environmental pressure groups continue to organise campaigns in the media and on-line, mainly to try to persuade governments to improve the emissions cuts they are making.

▼ Environmental activists from around the world shout slogans during a demonstration at the UN Climate Change Conference in Bali, 2007.

▶ Aqqaluk Lynge of the Inuit Circumpolar Council.

AN INCONVENIENT TRUTH

The documentary film *An Inconvenient Truth* was released in 2006. The film is the story of climate change. It was made by Al Gore, a former US vice president. After defeat to George W Bush in the 2000 presidential election, Gore decided to campaign on the dangers of climate change. The film was a box-office hit, and well-received by environmentalists and some scientists, and Gore shared the 2007 Nobel Peace Prize with the scientists of the IPCC. However, some of the film's content was controversial (see panel).

▼ Al Gore on his climate-change world tour.

ACTION FROM THE ARCTIC

Aqqaluk Lynge is president of the Inuit Circumpolar Council, which represents the people of the Arctic. He is a keen climate-change protestor, and raises awareness of the effect of climate change on the Arctic, such as loss of sea ice and poor hunting conditions. In 2007, Aqqaluk Lynge supported the Stop Stansted Airport Expansion campaign in the UK.

GET THE FACTS STRAIGHT

Al Gore's film was criticised because some of the science it contains is either incorrect or exaggerated. Much of its content, however, is recognised as accurate.

● The film suggests that the Gulf Stream is likely to stop flowing. An IPCC report states that this event is "very unlikely".

● The film claims that polar bears are drowning because of loss of Arctic sea ice. Evidence for this is unclear.

● The film claims that sea levels could rise by six metres "in the near future". This sort of rise will take hundreds of years at least.

AGAINST THE FLOW

DESPITE THE SCIENTIFIC EVIDENCE, there are still sceptics who do not believe that climate change is caused by human activities. Two of the sceptics' arguments are that today's climate change is natural, and that we can't tell what will happen in the distant future. These arguments are valid to some extent, but climate scientists do not think today's rapid climate warming can be natural.

▼ Gigantic volcanic eruptions send carbon dioxide into the atmosphere. This is Mount Pinatubo.

► Climate-change sceptics argue that heavy industry, such as steelmaking, doesn't unduly accelerate climate change.

NATURAL ARGUMENTS

Sceptics argue that, as the world's climate has been changing for millions of years, the current increase in global temperature must be a continuation of the same natural pattern. Among their theories are that climate change is caused by changes in the Sun's activity, or gases from volcanic eruptions. Computer climate models tell us that the Sun's activity does affect the climate, but that it is highly unlikely that they could cause the average global temperature increase we are seeing. And powerful volcanic eruptions do not emit as many greenhouses gases as human activities.

SCEPTICS IN THE MEDIA

Climate-change sceptics continue to argue their point in the media. They are given space in newspapers and on television because the media likes to give a balanced view of things (although some climate scientists think that the outnumbered sceptics get unfair coverage). An example was an article in 2007 in *New Statesman* magazine, entitled "Has Global Warming Stopped?" in which the author argued that because global temperatures have failed to rise for a few years, warnings of future climatic disaster were exaggerated. Another example was a UK television documentary entitled "The Great Climate Change Swindle", which set out reasons why evidence for change could not be trusted.

WHAT DO YOU THINK?

Sceptics argue that there is no link between carbon emissions and climate change.

■ Could current global warming be part of a natural cycle?

■ Is it worth taking a risk and taking no action to fight climate change?

■ Why do you think climate-change sceptics get so much coverage?

WITH A FEW SIMPLE ACTIONS everybody can reduce their carbon footprint significantly. Simple measures include turning off appliances when they are not needed, using energy-efficient light bulbs and other energy-efficient appliances (including washing machines and boilers), and turning down heating or air conditioning. We can also buy "green" electricity, walk or take public transport instead of driving, and stop flying.

▼ With urban growth like this, new buildings have to be designed to be energy efficient to reduce carbon emissions.

NON-FOSSIL ENERGY SOURCES

The next step is to reduce our dependence on fossil fuels by using a greater proportion of energy from renewable sources. These renewable sources include solar energy, wind energy, tidal energy and biofuels. Nuclear energy, although it has its own environmental problems, is also an option, and is being considered in several countries.

CLEAN COAL AND CARBON CAPTURE

We are stuck with coal-fired power stations for decades to come, and so new technology is needed to reduce carbon emissions from them. Clean-coal technologies include super-efficient power stations and carbon capture and storage (CCS). CCS systems will store carbon dioxide emissions deep underground rather than letting them into the atmosphere.

CARBON OFFSETS

A carbon offset is a way of paying for carbon emissions. For example, if you take a flight, you can pay for the carbon emissions from it to be offset elsewhere, perhaps for trees to be planted that will take up the carbon dioxide, or for an investment in renewable energy. However, you are not actually reducing your own carbon footprint.

Passenger aircraft engines are a major source of carbon dioxide. A return transatlantic flight for one person creates as much carbon dioxide as an average car does in a whole year. Frequent flyers have carbon footprints ten times the average. And emissions from aircraft have risen quickly because of budget airlines.

▼ Deforestation like this increases carbon emissions because trees absorb carbon dioxide. Planting new areas of forest can help.

◀ A demonstration against illegal logging.

PREDICTING THE FUTURE

CLIMATOLOGISTS work out what future climates might be like using climate models. These are extremely complex computer programs that simulate the Earth's atmosphere. The models work out what global temperatures and rainfall patterns could be in the future.

▼ Powerful computers, such as these ones at the UK's Met Office, create climate models.

FACING THE ISSUES

Climate change will affect how crops are grown across the world. The addition of carbon dioxide to the atmosphere will help crops to grow, but mostly in the world's richer countries. Many developing countries may lose some production because lower rainfall will leave them short of water. This could lead to serious food shortages if populations continue to grow in these developing countries.

MODEL PROBLEMS

The Earth's atmosphere is extremely complex, and climatologists don't completely understand how it works. For example, they don't really know how much carbon dioxide plants and oceans will soak up in future, or how increased temperatures will affect cloud cover. So climate models can never be totally accurate.

MODEL PREDICTIONS

Climate models predict that the average global temperature will continue to rise, by between 1°C and 6°C, depending on emissions. This will lead to an increase in heat waves. The temperature rise will also cause changes in rainfall patterns, with some areas getting more rain, and some areas less, leading to more floods and more droughts.

FUTURE EFFECTS OF CLIMATE CHANGE

Climate change is predicted to lead to numerous problems, such as deserts spreading in some places, the loss of coral reefs, melting permafrosts, the complete loss of Arctic sea ice, and changes in ocean currents. There could also be benefits as some agricultural areas may become more productive. But the picture is generally gloomy. Animals and plants that cannot adapt to changes quickly enough will die out. Perhaps the most serious change will be rises in sea levels because of expanding ocean water and melting ice caps. This could be anything up to a metre by 2100.

► This map shows how global temperatures could change in the northern hemisphere over the next century if carbon emissions stay at today's levels. The figures on the left are degrees of latitude north; the figures along the bottom are degrees of longitude. The colours show the possible temperature rise in degrees Celsius.

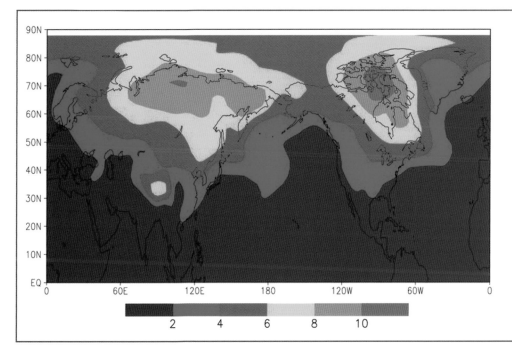

RESPONDING TO CLIMATE CHANGE

THE FIRST RESPONSE to climate change is to reduce carbon emissions, but even if we reduced carbon emissions to zero now, climate change would get more serious before it got better. It will take decades to reduce emissions, so we must be prepared for more extreme weather events such as floods and heat waves, changes in rainfall patterns, and sea-level rise. Sadly, the countries most likely to be affected by climate change are the poorest, and they are also the countries that produce the least greenhouse emissions.

▲ If climate change continues, we must prepare in advance for more extreme weather events such as this flood in Bangladesh.

PREPARATION

Examples of how we can prepare for the effects of climate change are improving coastal defences in places where sea-level rise will lead to more coastal flooding, such as building higher sea walls or planting mangroves to prevent erosion. Measures like this are possible in richer countries, but not always in developing countries.

ADAPTATION

The effects of climate change may be impossible to prepare for, in which case we will have to adapt to them. In the case of severe sea-level rise, coastal areas of many countries (such as Bangladesh) will become uninhabitable, and there are likely to be millions of refugees looking for new homes. In the worst-case scenario, with sea levels several metres above today's, large parts of major cities, such as London and New York, will have to be abandoned. Ultimately a runaway greenhouse effect can produce a climate like Venus where life is unsustainable.

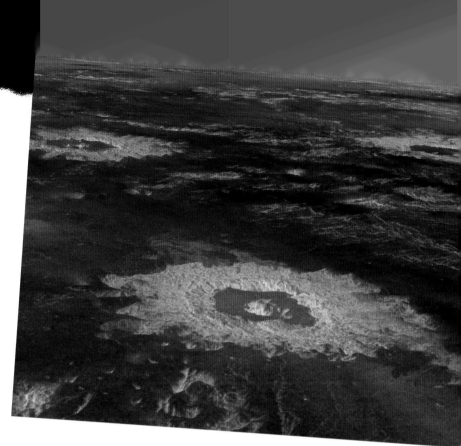

▲ The surface of Venus, where a runaway greenhouse effect has created temperatures of 465°C.

WHAT DO YOU THINK?

Climate change is the greatest challenge facing the human race today. The future of the planet as we know it is really under threat.

- Are you convinced that climate change is man-made?
- How do you think countries should respond to climate change?
- How are you responding to climate change yourself?
- Are you taking action to reduce your carbon footprint?

GLOSSARY

atmosphere: The layer of air that surrounds the Earth.

average global temperature: The average of all the long-term average air temperatures around the world.

carbon footprint: The amount of carbon dioxide a person or organisation puts into the atmosphere each year.

climate change: Changes in the world's climates, such as rising temperatures or increasing numbers of storms.

climate model: A computer simulation of the atmosphere that predicts what climate conditions are likely to be like in the future.

concentration: A measure of the amount of one material in a mixture of materials.

decomposing: Breaking down naturally into simpler chemicals.

developing country: A country in which the economy is changing from agricultural to industrial.

emissions: Gases that are given out when fossil fuels are burned, including carbon dioxide.

fossil fuels: Fuels made from the remains of animals and plants that died millions of years ago, such as coal, oil and gas.

glacier: A slow-flowing body of ice that flows downhill like an ice river.

global cooling: A cooling of the average global temperature.

global warming: The gradual warming of the atmosphere, caused by an increase in the greenhouse effect.

greenhouse effect: The natural effect where certain gases trap heat in the Earth's atmosphere.

greenhouse gas: One of the gases that traps heat in the atmosphere, and so is contributing to the greenhouse effect.

Gulf Stream: A warm ocean current that flows northwards in the Atlantic Ocean.

ice age: A cold period in the past when thick ice sheets advanced south to cover much of the northern hemisphere.

ice cap: A layer of ice many kilometres thick.

ice core: A sample of ice extracted from inside an ice cap.

IPCC: Abbreviation for the Intergovernmental Panel on Climate Change.

low-carbon technology: A technology that helps to reduce carbon emissions, such as wind turbines or carbon capture.

mid-latitudes: Regions of the world around halfway between the poles and the equator.

permafrost: Areas of ground close to the Arctic where the soil is permanently frozen.

radiate: To give out energy in rays or waves.

renewable sources: A source of energy that does not rely on burning fossil fuels, such as solar cells and wind turbines.

summit: Meeting of government leaders.

water vapour: The gas form of water, formed when water evaporates or boils.

Websites

www.metoffice.gov.uk
Official site of the UK's Meteorological Office, with interesting sections on the greenhouse effect and climate change.

www.noaa.gov/climate.html
Climate section of the USA's National Oceanic and Atmospheric Administration.

www.ipcc.ch
Home of the Intergovernmental Panel on Climate Change, including summaries of their reports.

www.ukcip.org.uk/
Home page of the UK's Climate Impacts Programme, which discusses how climate change could affect British people.

www.foei.org/en/campaigns/climate
The climate change section on the Friends of the Earth website.

www.greenpeace.org/international
Homepage of Greenpeace International, with details of Greenpeace's climate-change campaigns.

INDEX

Here are the lists of contents for each title in *Science in the News*:

CLIMATE CHANGE

WHAT IS CLIMATE CHANGE? • CLIMATE CHANGE SCIENCE • CLIMATE SCIENCE HISTORY
CLIMATE CHANGE IN THE PAST • CAUSES OF CLIMATE CHANGE • CARBON DIOXIDE EMISSIONS
THE EFFECTS OF CLIMATE CHANGE • CLIMATE CHANGE REPORTS • PIONEER PRESSURE GROUPS
CLIMATE-CHANGE SUMMITS • GOVERNMENT REACTIONS • NEW INDUSTRIAL NATIONS
CONTINUING PROTESTS • AGAINST THE FLOW • CARBON REDUCTION • PREDICTING THE FUTURE
RESPONDING TO CLIMATE CHANGE

ORGAN TRANSPLANTATION

INTRODUCTION • IN THE BEGINNING • WORLD FIRSTS • ORGAN CRISIS • PRESUMED CONSENT
LIFE FROM LIFE • RELIGION & CULTURE • ARTIFICIAL ORGANS • XENOTRANSPLANTATION
STEM CELL RESEARCH • THE RIGHT TO AN ORGAN? • TRANSPLANT TOURISTS • ORGAN SELLERS
REGULATING THE TRADE • POST-OPERATIVE LIFE • FACE TRANSPLANTS • NEW BREAKTHROUGHS

COSMETIC SURGERY

INTRODUCTION • ANCIENT ORIGINS • THE FIRST AND SECOND WORLD WARS
FROM HOLLYWOOD TO THE HIGH STREET • SURGICAL TREATMENTS • NON-SURGICAL TREATMENTS
THE BENEFITS • THE RISKS • SURGERY ADDICTS • TEENAGE SURGERY • CHECKS AND BALANCES
THE SURGEONS • VIEWING FIGURES • "THE BEAUTY MYTH" • BOOM AND BUST
ALTERNATIVES • FACING THE FUTURE

NUCLEAR POWER

WHAT IS NUCLEAR POWER? • THE HISTORY OF NUCLEAR POWER
WHO USES NUCLEAR POWER? • NUCLEAR FUELS • NUCLEAR POWER STATIONS • NUCLEAR REACTOR TYPES
NUCLEAR POWER FOR TRANSPORT • NUCLEAR WASTE • BUILDING AND DECOMMISSIONING
NUCLEAR SAFETY • THE CHERNOBYL DISASTER • TERROR THREATS • ROGUE STATES
ANTI-NUCLEAR CAMPAIGNS • NUCLEAR POWER PLANS
NUCLEAR FUSION • THE NUCLEAR FUTURE

GENETICS

GENETIC MODIFICATION • DARWIN – FROM MONKEY TO MAN • IN THE GENES
A MASTER-RACE – A BREED APART? • ANIMAL ODDITIES • DNA – A CODE FOR LIVING
THE CHANGING CODE • RECESSIVE GENES – A HIDDEN INHERITANCE • ARE GM CROPS FRANKENSTEIN FOODS?
DANGEROUS MEDDLING? • MAKING MONSTERS? • "GENETIC FINGERPRINTS" • TRACING YOUR ROOTS• NATURE AND NUTURE
ALTERED INHERITANCE • CLONING – A CARBON COPY? • A LEGACY OR TIMEBOMB?

MAKING A NEW LIFE

CREATING LIFE • THE MAGIC OF LIFE • MOTHERS AND SONS • ARTIFICIAL INSEMINATION
PARENTAL RESPONSIBILITY • IVF – THE TEST TUBE BABY • MULTIPLE PREGNANCIES • THE GIFT OF LIFE
SURROGACY – TWO MOTHERS? • TOO OLD FOR PARENTHOOD? • CHECKING PROGRESS
SONS OR DAUGHTERS? • SAVIOUR SIBLINGS • FROZEN FOR THE FUTURE • WHAT IS A CLONE?
HUMAN CLONES • CREATING LIFE IN THE FUTURE